Chiaroscuro

Chiaroscuro

Grey Graffiti of a Complex Mind

Dhruv Sharma

PARTRIDGE
A Penguin Random House Company

Print information available on the last page.

To order additional copies of this book, contact
Partridge India
000 800 10062 62
orders.india@partridgepublishing.com

www.partridgepublishing.com/india

Contents

This book is dedicated to all the people who gave me enough confidence and memories – the two drivers, to make this happen.

Acknowledgment

This book is a result of complex emotions that run through all of our minds and some wonderful support of wonderful people. I would like to thank all these lovely people.

First and foremost, I would like to thank my mother who always believed in me, inspired me and tried to understand me. Thank you!

I would like to thank Ms. Tasneem Mohammed for being a continuous support to me. Your valuable words and suggestions have been the driving force.

I would also like to thank Mr. Laxminarayan Gupta for prodding me to take a concrete step with my poems.

Mr. Abhineet Tomar, for providing those wonderful images, I am thankful to you.

Mr. Jeric Romano, who patiently listened to all my queries and again helped me in the development of this book, I am grateful to you.

Mr. Nikhil Jain, Mr. Shobhit Shrivastava, Ms. Shreya Gupta, and all my friends and colleagues, thanks for driving me to write more.

And finally, I would like to thank my family, who were and are always there with me. I love you.

Introduction

Mind is a complex maze. Entangled with varieties of emotions, it colors the canvass with different shades. And the final painting, displays a picture that most of us, at least subconsciously could identify. Bringing out different layers of this mind, this book projects some of the manifold moods active or dormant in this beautiful machinery called the human mind.

Hope you relate with some of the shades.

I am no one but your reflection.

Interstices

This closed space
An amalgamation of rooms
Occupying in its heart
An ineffable gloom
This ramshackle building
Devoid of any norms
This building of bricks
People call my home
Appears strange to me
In all its forms
Every single time I enter into
This haunted dorm

I can hear the sounds
My ears fail to catch
I can sense an air
My senses fail to match
But I believe
I surely can perceive
That this haunting
Replete with everything
Is in fact incomplete

May be it's the doors
Suggesting me a thing
Before swishing into dark
Or it's the windows
Continuously rattling
Scribbling their mark
To give a hint
Which I cannot understand
But I surely can feel

The presence of someone
Not being present

It's then I realize
It's the damp walls
Withered and covered
With chinks and blots
Ricocheting and presenting
The laughs, the chatters
The duels, the quarrels
In this haunting without a ghost

And now when a single ghoul
In me is only left here
These walls
Damped and moistened
With the tears of yours
Try to break free
Try to leave me
To join you
And they shout out loud
Tearing their skins apart
By uttering cries
In the form of interstices
The deep crevices
Formed from our voices
And are reminders of our choices
To part

And it's then I conclude
That I am not alone
But I am surrounded
By the weeping, crying walls
Filled with the cracks
The deep interstices
Of our agonies

Afterlife

Attached with emotions
Leashed with relations
I lie down motionless
No place do I go
But I keep wavering
Oscillating to and fro

I keep thinking
Wasting myself
Over the issues
Important yet trivial
Real yet unreal
In this world
Like everyone else
Fighting over some cause
That shadows my presence

Amid these dregs
I too am a residue
Like other sediments
I too have to pay my due
I have to answer
I have to address
I too have to live
And die in congress

Careers, relationships
Love, friendships
Highs, lows
Feats, blows
Success, failures
Catalysts, barriers

I've always been around them
Defined by them
Troubled by them
Confined by them
And like any other deposit
I rot, I blot
For I am not
Singular, myself
But I am just a mirage
Of every other sediment

But now I've to be free
I've to be a cloud
I've to be stringless
I've to hold no shroud
I want to be released
I want to flow
I want to leave
I want to glow
I want to detach
From every trivial cause
I want to separate
From every logical clause

No checks, no boundaries
Will then hold my flight
No plague, no heartbreak
Will then become my plight
For I will be no dreg
But a distant star
I will be spotless
Without any scar

But I am not illogical
I am not insane
My answers have logic

The solution is always sane
But I know the fear
I know the pain
That curbs my leap
To meet the answer
The ultimate solution
Again and again

And as I decompose here
Like everyone else
I pray to God
To give me wings
So that I curb the swings
And leap into the sea
Where I can detach
My identity
My singularity
From these dregs
And see myself
As ethereal
Real and surreal
As an air
That you can feel
You can breathe
But cannot see

I want to go
I want to leave
And one day
I believe
I will jump
And I will leave
Only to start anew
A beautiful afterlife

The Man inside me

The man inside me
An escapist
A hopeless romantic
Lives in his world of romance
A world of exotic trance
A world of ecstasy
Far from any practicality

The man inside me
A delusional loon
A poltroon
Shuts the doors of reality
Denies his ear to rationality
But accepts only the imagery
The imagery he has drawn
Beautiful yet brittle
To survive the strikes of brawn

The man inside me
An idle dreamer
A fantasiser
He continuously weaves
His blanket of guise,
He duly believes
The oppressed lies
The lies he preserves
He nurtures
Safe in this haven
He calls his heaven

The man inside me
An escapist

A complex pacifist
Pays heed to no tocsins
No shouts, no jeers
But ignorantly he cheers
His stay in the world
The world with congenial relationships
Without any conflicts

The man inside me
A professor
A shy confessor
Happily thrives
In his sublime universe
For he lives with a surety
That no one can snatch
His love, his thoughts
His pictures, his images

But the expriences of life
Wisdom that made him wise
Makes him aacknowledge the truths
The truths that he is misfit
His life is a fabricated skit
And this knowledge
Threatens the very existence
Of the treasure
Of the myth
His imagery, his works
On which his world is based

And in a futile battle
Which he ultimately will lose
He fights hard
To avoid the noose
And clinging on the shards

The shards of lies
The beautiful lies
He thought he will never lose
The man inside me
An escapist
A hopeless romantic
Wins himself
By losing himself
And he's born
After being dead
To die again

Shore

Amid the maelstrom of currents
These monstrous waves
Keep slapping me
Keep swatting me
Trying to keep me down

And clinging on a dinghy
I do feel too feeble
Too helpless
To support my own weight
In this vast, terrifying blue

But then suddenly
My sinking eyes glue
To a distant sight
To a dwindling shore
Where
Some hands are reaching out for me
Some bodies are rooting for me
Some eyes are concerned for me
Some faces are anxious for me

And I see the faces and the mouths
The lips and the jaws
Vigorously moving up and down
Supposedly shouting the language
Of struggle and motivation
Trying very hard
To actuate me to swim
But not to sink
In this unwelcoming current

And despite being thrashed
Being continuously squashed
As a traitor by these raiders
I keep swimming
I keep clinging
In a hope to reach out
To those concerned people
Standing on the shore

Abhineet Fotografie

People across Borders

Wired to rate
Programmed to discriminate
We were born
Breathing an air
That did propagate
This strong feeling of hate
For the people
Who were not ours

Bashing was innate
Hatred did inflate
We cheered for the grim
For the spokes
Belonging to a different rim
As we believed
That these people conceived
Different, opposing
Rebelling, appalling
Ideas
That our rationale
Our intellectual
Refused to cover

Our hatred got the fuel
From every single duel
And we kept thriving
We kept riding
On this wave
Where we were proud
To demolish
But just weren't ready
To replenish

This arid with love

But then
The bridges abridged
The contact was made
We saw our misconceptions
Slowly fade
We saw our reflections
In almost every single face
Wishing to make
His home, a beautiful place

We all root for the Hero
And boo the villain
We all support the cause
And protest the omen
We stood on the same side
When we thought we weren't
We all were same
When we thought we were different

I know the trend to hate
Still thrives
But the frail trail of love
Also survives
In the hearts
Who want to supplant
The raven with dove
The hate with love
And my eyes
Once rigid, and livid
Are now vivid
For they see
My enemies, my foes
Across the boundaries
Behind the LOCs

Colored
In the same colors
My families, my friends
Are colored in

The House

Living in the sheds of a hut
I witness often
The acid torrents
Burning and marring
The once innocuous faces
Into spectral images
Images disfigured
Images unfit
To be assimilated
Into the high social class

And often in this dire transformation
Of harmless into harmful
I check the rashes on my skin
The green burns
That these disparaging
These slandering
These butchering torrents
Gave me
And rendered me
Morally disabled
For the rest of my life

I agree
That my actions might have been childish
My acts might have been foolish
But no act of mine
No harmless action of mine
I believe
Deserved this castigation
This scorching process of chastening me

In the name of your demigods
The cults you follow

I know
I've been imperfect
I've been flawed
I am no close to your standard of best
The perfect alpha
But being a simple man
A man as insignificant as you
I believe
I didn't deserve
These quips of whips
That ultimately pommeled my back
So bad
That now I am crippled
And doomed forever

Now, in these thunderstorms
When I see the other reflections
Getting slandered and murdered
Brutally and sadistically
By your callous terms
I do want to step out
And get greased with your germs
By empowering these men
With the swords of poisons
To fight off your slander
With the slander of my own

But when the contusion becomes green
My zeal is also preened
And helpless I then shout
To call these men into my house
For this house is secure
Immune to these attacks

For the bricks of this mansion
Are made of ego
That protects me
A crippled, disfigured me
From this poisonous sham

Lights

When the entire world
Is bright
Is Illuminated
With different lights
Different colors
Happy faces
Merry eyes,
My eyes
Disguise
To show others
That I am happy
Content, revel
Merry and vivid
But these happy eyes
Covering my lies
Still craving for you
Want to see nothing but you

I don't want others
To apprise
That I am sad
I don't want others
To surmise
Various theories
Various facts
I don't want to be in blue
In gloom
But my eyes
My heart
Knows what's true
As there is no room
No light
When I don't see you.

And amid this light
The sparkling sky
The vivid houses
And the beautiful faces
My heart still wants
To go to the ways
The paths
Leading to your home
In a hope
To see you once
Just once
Your smiling, lovely
Beautiful, lustrous
Bright face
In these lights

I know it's unwise
Not to take the advice
To ignore her
But my heart is all dark
Dismal
Ashen
And even the festival
Of lights
Brings no relief
As there is no light
Without this belief
That you were mine
Rather it reminds me
More of you
And more of the fact
My heart
Everyday endures
That you are not near
That you are gone

Lovers

There at some distant view
Two people
Inebriated with elixir of one other
Unaware of the noises
Of the noisy world
Peacefully sit and wear
The tranquil reflection
Of a tranquil lake

And sitting on this becnch
With sometimes breeze
And other times the sounds of leaves
Interrupting the scene
She leans over
And puts her head
On my shoulder
And glancing upwards
With her questioning eyes
Peaceful but troubled eyes
Interrogates for the answers

She keeps studying my face
Scanning with her deep eyes
And answers herself
Her doubts
Which now are also mine
With an enticing smile
An assurance
That she's with me
And everything is fine

Continuously addressing
Continuously pressing

Her palms on my hands
She rests her peace
My peace, our peace
Her confidence
My confidence, our confidence
All on my sturdy arms

Gleefully she keeps staring
She keeps speaking
In a language
Only to me
Asking me
To arrest her
Forever
In this moment
In this picture
Of love

Being enticed
With this picturesque moment
In this picturesque life
I suspend my beliefs
Only to believe
In a world of her love
My love, Our love

And sitting motionless
Lost in her dreams
In the gateways of her eyes
In the serenity of her face
I sit motionless with her
In my own world

Annoying, Badgering
Gauche passersby
Soon disturbs

Soon irks
This perfect symphony
With their callous cacophony
Exhorting me to rise
And close the gates
To protect her
To protect myself

But as I rise
To clear off this cries
I find she's gone
Vanished in thin air
And awake, disgruntled
I now have to find a place
A distant space
To recall
To reunite
To restart living her
The present in present
The perfect image
With an open eyed slumber
At some other distant view
On some other bench

Bitter Buds

No sugar tastes sweet
For all my buds are bitter
No answer seems complete
For all my thought is litter

No light represents bright
For my eyes are all dark
No celebration goes alight
For my presence leaves no mark

No symphony sounds dulcet
For my ears have gone humdrum
No vista appears perfect
For my mind is in conundrum

No words of praise soothe me long
For my personality is so dented
No feats of success make me strong
For my psyche is too demented

But being a mortal of clay
I still long to find a way
To a tangible paradise
Where my psyche can rise
From the dregs of toxic waste

But then
My lungs are filled with poisons
My bronchi is covered with toxins
My eyes have sunken dour
My voice has become sour

And even though I long to taste
The sugary treat
I see my desire going waste
For there is no sweet
In the once sweet sugar
Sugar that is now made bitter
By my sullen taste buds

Hoyden

A hoyden met me
In an old country tavern
She plucked the beats of sound
As the evening turned seven

She barraged with a force
Assailed my old cavern
I tried to camouflage
But was trapped in her raven

She stomped onto my chest
And pulled me off the roof
I tried to see my stars
But I could no longer be aloof

She asked me with an askance
A look of dirt in her eyes
I tried to hide myself
But I couldn't cover my lies

A centurion in the battle
She flowed like a gale
I tried again to be aloft
But my sobriety was all impaled

By the time it was nine
I undressed my robe of blush
I tanned my skin with her hue
I shouted her name in hush

The floor was a centrifuge
The flat became all round

But the soul nevertheless unrestrained
Kept dancing on your sound

My eyes didn't move an inch
They followed all her moves
My legs made my bosom dance
In the circles of her grooves

Exhilarated with the passion
I forgot it was now eleven
But mind still high on her drug
Kept moving like it was seven

In the alien humdrum of madness
She slipped into the dark of night
Her shadow became a silhouette
The hoyden vanished from my sight

My dancing legs came to halt
The unfettered soul wore its fetters
The script of zeal was stained
As the ink spilled on the letters

Exhausted, I gazed up now
The grim watch still showed eleven
The troglodyte's soul re-emerged
As I head back to my cavern

Behind my plain smile

Pain is in my heart
Smile is on my face
I do carry a grin
Throughout this emotional daze

Days
I know they're gone
Those lovely days
Those beautiful times
With chimes
Of beautiful rhymes
Those mesmerizing days
Those splendid nights
I know they're gone
I wear now only the burns
I borne

I juggle my emotions
My sorrows
My throes
My anxieties
All in disdain
But I do ingrain
A plain grin
While I fade away
In this phase

I am not ignorant
I am not inane
I am not a fool always
I know the faces of truth
I know the facts

The grim facts
I have experienced the slashes
The slashes of sword
That cut my dreams
My aspirations, my hopes
Into tiny little pieces

But I still fight
I still find ways
To resurrect
To efface
The burns and scars
And restructure
My dangling frame
My burning name

And even if it takes a toll
On my emotional health
I very well know
The ball is no longer in my court
And I smile
With tears in my eyes
Whenever she asks
Whether I am alright?

Do you know?

Do you know?
You are the one
Who holds the key
Of happiness for me

Do you know?
You are the reason
Behind my grin
Behind my felicity
For you are my
Only source of ecstasy

Do you know?
The kites of hope
Fly high
In the sky of mirth
Of joy, of delight
Whenever you are in my sight

Do you know?
I love to be in a world
Where there's me
Where there are you
Where everything is beautiful
And nothing is blue

Do you know?
The first time I saw you
I was magnetized
I was mesmerized
I felt something inside

That the simple words
Couldn't completely describe

Do you know?
There's something in you
That pulls me through
From the grim
To a world
Where I leave
All the pain, all the bane
And sing my heart out
In this magical joy of rain

Do you know?
I fear to lose you
For you are special
You are important
You are to me
Like my almighty's present

Do you know?
I think of you
Every second, every minute
Every single moment
Without any control over myself
And I just want to tell you
That you, my sweet
are my absolute need
And I miss you

Rain

Dancing on their own beats
The lovely showers
Along with the gentle zephyr
Touch me
Poke me
Ask me out
To meet them
Greet them
In a way
They meet me
They greet me
And I do oblige
I do provide
Myself
As I come out
To meet the sublime
To feel the rhyme
Of this beautiful feel
That helps me deny
The conventions
And be me
That helps me defy
The reservations
And be free
From the cerebrals
The intellectuals
Sitting inside
Waiting for the rain
They view as a storm
To subside

Where's the End

I stand there
On the dead end
Thinking
Where I have to go next?
Is this the end?
The end of the bay
The thing that drove me
Night and day

I don't know
If this is the call
To halt my quest
To reach out to you
And rest
Or to continue
My march
Until I try everything
Until I give my all
Until I give my best?

Perplexed, lost
I stand there
Confused, fray
I try to find a way
To the next decision
To take
To the next move
To make

But all my eyes can see
Are some blurred lines
Which show a mirage

An illusion
And the usual me
Astringent and stern
I stand there
Without knowing what to do
Whether to advance
Or retract back home
I cannot decide
As there is a wall
A high, very high wall
Of fears, of apprehensions
Blocking all my movements

And here I
Stand
Looking out
For the better alternates
Sounding conclusions
But I couldn't move an inch
Cause I know
My directions
My journey
Starts with
And ends at
You

And when I cannot see you
My eyes desperately
Search for a road
To walk
But they couldn't advance
They couldn't depend
On the sight
On the vista they see
For the roads are all obviated
And the hopes are deleted

And my eyes
Searching through this labyrinth
Move but couldn't make me walk
For they simply don't know
Where's the end?

Blizzard

This life
An arena of opportunities
A venue of uncertainties
A farm of probabilities
An avenue of possibilities
Has so many colors
So many flavors
True adventures
To offer
To make my life
Excitingly haphazard
In the blizzard
I chose to walk in
But still
I fancy an idea
Of walking
Quietly
Peacefully
With you
Along the boulevard
Of my life

Equation

Trying to solve this equation
Containing variables
Of different tracks
Often I fail to grasp
The difference between
Contacts and Contracts
For every word I hear
I assume to be true
I preserve these figments
I see them as some clue
To help me solve
The puzzle
The riddle
Of my misery
Which I often fail to grasp

Sometimes I emulate
To replicate
Images of emotions
One produces
Sometimes I estimate
To speculate
Magnitude of reactions
One induces

Sometimes I intimate
My findings
To get them accepted
As a logical solution
Sometimes I simulate
My experiments

To find one truth
In all the resolutions

I keep experimenting
I keep publishing
Different ideas
Different theories
And when I think
I've solved the mystery
The source of my misery
The enigma of dark
Questions manifold
The expression reappears
The satisfaction disappears

Being defeated
I realize
That my works
My experiments
They all are futile
For I am a reflection
Of the people I detest
Of the notions I protest
Of the facts I deny
Of the conventions I decry

Lying in the dark
I see myself
No different from you
For I too accept
I too reject
For I too am flawed
I too am odd
Simply a fraud
Just like you
And there in this abyss

This unholy pit
Devoid of any definition
Of reason
Of truth
We rot
Together

All I wanted

All I wanted
Was a minute or two
Of you
But you were never there
To care
To listen to the things
I wanted to share
And my anticipating heart
Wearing a smile
Kept waiting
All the while
To have you
Here
Near me
But you never showed up
You never came
While I kept waiting
Foolishly to find your name

Scarecrow

Summers and winters
Autumns and springs
I take on everything
Mother Nature brings
And I stand still
To oblige, to fulfill
The task, the duty
My master, my lord
Assigned me
To protect his land
The field of the great maven
I thus have to fight
With many a raven

Day and night
I stand still
I stand motionless
This piece of land
Is my permanent address
My day
Starts with auroral rays
My night
Dissolves in the cold daze

I stand still
I show no movement
Even when my nose runs down
Or my legs catch blight
For my aim, my ultimate reason
Is to stand upright
Keeping my lean and lank
Yet resolute stature, tight

I thus strive to do my work right

I stand still
I show no movement
In any torrent
In any rain
For I feel obliged
That master has chosen me
That master has trusted me
With this honorable duty
And I thus duly
Withstand dust and rime
Endure all these hard times
And absorb all the pain

I stand still
I show no movement
But never had I complained
About the straw hair
About the rags
The tatters, I am dressed in
And that worn out hat
That always has been
Over my head
But I feel
That sense of scare
That gloomy feeling
When master doesn't care
To show his affection
His concern, his love
Which is far above
Any price

At times
I even would like to run
To make a call

To voice my emotions
My overwhelming sentiments
But standing here for decades
Has made my muscles numb
I thus can do nothing
But wait for him
For his one call of love

All I genuinely want
Is a loving hand
A gentle pat
On my shoulder
That will remove the boulder
Of the pains
Of the stains
My tatters sported
During every hardship

So I still stand here
Doing my job sincerely
To scare away
The marauders
And I wish
To hear soon the swish
Of the golden crop
That would brighten up
His face
And then maybe
He could come up to me
And shower a little praise
A little love
I always long for

Oh Almighty!

Thou art the shade
Where I want to perch
Thou art the joy
I've always searched
Thy is the power
Oh Majesty
The Lord of Lords
The Ultimate Ruler
The Supreme Healer
That enlightens
That brightens
The palest of souls
The gravest of ghouls
And transform them
Into seekers of truth
Seekers of peace
Seekers of thou
Oh Almighty

I've lurched enough
In the labyrinth of lust
I've searched enough
The paraphernalia of rust
But,
Oh Savior of souls
The Gardener of hopes
The Creator of dreams
The Architect of sheens,
I want to stop this race
On you gate, Oh Just
For thou art the force
The Purest

Oh Divine
Thou art the panacea
Who'll stop me combust
And make my soul refine

The benevolent
The magnificent
Heal my weary wounds
Color my dreary life
With thy cerulean blue
Oh Majestic one
I am standing here
Still, motionless
For thou to mold me
And make me thy own
Make me the one
For the One

A book

I've written a book
Keeping you in mind
I've placed it near you
It's not that hard to find
All my feelings
My emotions
My thoughts
My sentiments
I've written in it
You'll find
Your sketch
Your portrait
Your description
From my eyes
Bit by bit

Search in the pages
You'll find the key
To the only answer
I want you to see
As the only answer
The only solution
To every question
To every problem
Is nothing else but you
That I've written
I've painted
I've decorated
In all these pages
Of my book

Crazy

I am crazy
For I want to be crazy
In this civilized looking
Crazy world
Doing all the crazy things
All the crazy play
With a crazy way

I am crazy
For I believe
It's fun
To be a crazy one
I am crazy
To be intentional
In breaking the conventional
I am crazy
To laugh
Scream
Like a maniac
I am crazy
To talk and do
Whatever I like
Without applying the logics
And the reasons

I am crazy
To listen to my heart
And do it all
My way
My style
As this craziness
This naughtiness

Is the thing
That brings me a smile
And I have no guilt
No interest
To act mannered
To act sane
For this decorum
Just doesn't contain
The pure joy
My heart wants to fondle
And live with

I may appear serious
I may appear grave
But trust me
I am crazy
I am mad
I am insane
A complete muddlehead
But I love this way
To go against the flow
To show
The crazy, very crazy side of me
For I want to experience
The glee
The puerility
The credulity
Of a child
A crazy child

A song of solace

Voice of the silence
Song of the solace
Is now a preface
Of the story
In my case
As echo is now a song
I had known all along
I made it a choice
To make silence my voice

My opinions now
Are my narrations
My imaginations now
Are my conversations
The reverb
Is now my sound
My solace in grim
Is now unbound

Echo is what I rejoice
As silence is my true voice
Solitude is now a salvation
Void is now my destination
Solace is now my muscle
In the world of hustle
For this world
Never empathized
Never realized
Never understood
Never read
My heart spurring emotions
My core asking care

My soul seeking love
My mind reciting prayers

Thus
Amidst the rush
I find this solitude
My own place
This silence
A true grace
And without any strain
Any expectation
I embrace
This face
Of mine
As I sing
My song
My song of solace

Alluring Death

You are dark
You are evil
You are blasphemous
You are morally black
Yet there is an enigma
A mystery
A beauty
A curiosity
To know you
To see with the eyes
The definitions of true
As everything
In your proximity enchants
Asks me to advance
Inside the black
The abysmal hollow
That inevitably follows
The truth
For you are truth
You are forever

I see in you
Oh darkness in blue
A beautiful damsel
An enchantress
Longing to hold me
Support me
Forever
In her arms
But ironically I run
I cannot come
When I want us

To be one
For I am gripped
In the shackles
Of the intellectual qualms
But I do want to be
In the pack
I do want to follow
Your track
I do want to meet you
Greet you
With a smile
My fate
My end

Cupid's Arrow

Again
This has happened to me
When someone's presence
Made me glee

Again
Someone stepped into
My world of imagination
Again
Someone rose
My level of expectation

Again
Someone adorned my dream
Again
I hope to cross the stream

Again
Someone has become special
Someone has become prime
Again
Sounds in the air
Are filled with melodious chimes

Again
Songs make some meaning
Born are new feelings
Again
Heart has started believing
And burgeon the old seedlings

Again
I wish
To believe my insight
That everything will be
Perfect and bright

Again
I hope
To see green
To make the scene
Bright and sheen

Again I have kept a green heart
inside me
and wait for the bird
to perch

Again I sit back
Wearing the smile
And singing the songs
The songs of mirth

Thus my search
From nadir to zenith
Never ends
And my urge
to purge
the maladies
Grow and grow
And again
Oh Lord!
Not again
I am struck
With a Cupid's arrow

Trace

Fixated on the window
My eyes
Search thoroughly
For any sign
Of your presence

Always beside the walls
My ears
Wait anxiously
For any knock
Or footfall
To happen

But there was nothing changed
All the signs
All the marks
Remains unaltered
Unstained
But still
I hold the pretense
That this absence
Will not be for long

And thus
Despite being frail
I allay
My impatient heart
With a false parable
That if I cannot
Trace your mark
You surely
Will be able to track me

From the trails
I have left
And I am still leaving
At every station
At every nook
I walk on
For you to find me
For me to find you

Nameplate

Isolated, quarantined
Is my identity
In the social warfare
In this swank society
Which declares
Itself filled with flair
Which cannot be compared
The visions surely are impaired

What these ostentatious souls
Can't predict and understand
Is the caliber, the power
of the mighty human hand

It's the power of this hand
Which conquers the land
Which transforms dud into grand
Which makes the bland, brand

So let the blows come
I am ready to rise
I will never reflect any glum
And will never compromise.

It's the time now
To relate and conflate
The powers, the traits
To write, to create
The story of my fate
Which soon will be written
In my Nameplate

Ponder

Ponder
Oh mortal
Ponder
Ponder where the wings have gone?
Who curtailed your dreams?
What made you fall?

Ponder
Oh corporeal
Ponder
Ponder where the twinkle is lost?
Who stole your dream?
What made you appalled?

Ponder
Oh earthling
Ponder
Ponder why the stream is so dull?
Why your reflection is cloudy?
Why is your presence annulled?
Ponder
Oh human being
Ponder
Ponder why that self is hurt?
Who appropriated your smile?
Why are you so dismantled?

Ponder
Oh friend
Ponder
Ponder who's the culprit?

Tell me the name of the swindler
And I will make him submit

Ponder
Oh dear
Ponder
Ponder who's at the fault?
Tell me the name of the sinister
And I will make him lachrymose
Ponder
Oh helpless
Ponder
Ponder and give me the answer
I am brandishing my sword
And I am ready to slaughter

Ponder
Oh reflection
Ponder
Ponder and give me some name
I know I only am the felon
But now I want to shift the blame

Her deep irises

Far away from the house of glass
Her black, deep iris, slides
Into a pond of magical waves
She rides on the neap tides

She amass the jellies on the beach
She savors the flavors of peach
She writes her name on the sand
She ambles on this hinterland

She flirts with the mischievous winds
She flows with the imperious gale
She dances with the cold waters
She blithely makes her sail

She rests on the cold sands
And counts the stars of night
She makes pictures, she draws faces
She wears the perfume of delight

Apparently happy and lost
With her head down
I ask for her name
And give her a wakeup call

Awaken from her slumber
She tries hard to encumber
The lovely sights
Inside the shutters of eyes
But I furtively catch a glimpse
Of those exclusive films
That her deep, black irises

Unknowingly apprise
Unwillingly describe
The more of the beauty
That lies in her

Unspoken words

Little are the things said
Little are the things heard
Little are the things expressed
These emotions are wordless

These wordless talks
These unspoken emotions
Spell a cast over me
As they are making me
To loose myself
Completely
Absolutely.

For I am losing
All the control
Over my heart
Over my soul
As getting you
Being close to you
Every second
Every moment
Looks like my only goal

Sure, I know
The unspoken eyes
Of yours
Speak everything
I want to listen
So why do you refrain
Yourself
Give me no other clue
I know something is there

In your heart too
Speak your heart to me
Speak in your voice
And make me dance
make me fall in trance

Your silence kills me
Speak your heart out
For you will see then
The way the things will work out
Drop this arrogance
Or ignorance
which keeps us apart
For you know
You are in mine
And I am in your heart

So say yes
And open the gate
To happiness
Which will dowse you
Which will souse me
Which will shower upon us
Like a rain of joy
As you will be my girl
And I will be your boy
And forever we will enjoy
The life we will write
The life we will employ

Dead leaves on the road

Scattered all over
The road
Were these dead leaves
Which showed
Colors of brown
Hopes slumped down
As they rot
In despair thoughts
And hopeless they lie
In their slumber
For they were nothing
More than a lumber

Suddenly they heard
A distant noise
They opened their eyes
To find it's a voice
From a car approaching
Swiftly encroaching

These ashen leaves
Were all geared
As this car
Was coming near
Their faces glow
As they had a hope
To flow with the gust
That will provide
Fuel for their ride
To come out
From the feel
When they died

And came the car
Came the gust
They jumped
They flowed
With the adhering dust
They had their moments
To enjoy
To share
As they were out
From their snare

But small was the flight
And long was the plight
Soon were they
Back to mound
As their hopes were
Back to ground

And fallen were their hopes
Which depend on
Mercy of others
And crestfallen
And haggard
They returned
To their trance
As they wait
For their chance
To break the cuffs
To break the chains
And this cycle repeats
Again and again

Mistakes

I've made mistakes
I've made so many that
I have lost the count
There is no number
No measure
To illustrate
The stupid trait
Innate
That made me
And makes me
Do the same
Over and over again

All the stupidities
All the imbecilities
I made
Exemplifies
The amount of aspiration
The paramount desperation
The hopeless expectation
The characteristic frustration
Along with
So many blemishes
I constitute
In a not so perfect
Mind of mine

But always
There has been
Preponderance of optimism
That I will act smart
And I will mend

The flaws in me
I will rectify
All the broken bridges
All the broken trust
So that everything
Can become re workable
And life re lovable

But not every mistake
Gives you a second chance
To make
Things work fine
For the stakes
The bounds
Then reach to the heights
To some level
Where my speech
My hands
Can never reach
Which then
Reminds me
That I've made a mistake
For which there is no remedy.

Odyssey

Stand
Don't be afraid
Walk
Your way is yet to be made
Face
For the fight has begun
Run
For the time has come
Survive
You don't have to fade
Thrive
You are your only aid
Believe
You have to glide
Abide
Make your own stride
Face
All the phase of glum
Move
You cannot be numb
Challenge
All those against you
Prove
No one can be you
Endure
All the slaps of destiny
Rise
From the phase of agony
Embrace
The downhill in your way
Hope
There is always a ray

Smile
If you ever fall
Listen
To your ultimate call
Play
Your rules your way
Win
Make your own day
Remember
Your zeal will take you through
Proceed
Nobody can ever stop you

Subtle Vestiges

Content
With the potpourri
Of everyday flavors
The perfume
Of poignant love
Invades
And pervades
The regular curry
Of complacency
With the fumes of spark
A whiff of charm
A sniff of romance
That is lost
In the gait
Of our everyday lives
And then
These subtle vestiges
Make the people
Fly again
Relive again
Fall to fall again
In a beautiful essence
People call love
Even when the inevitable
Predetermined fate
Awaits

Romantic Lines

Sipping up the wine
I see your eyes
A million times
To see that shine
That made me numb
I hum those stupid lines
To catch the rhyme
To make the time
But I end up
Looking dumb

I try to express
I try to impress
To get a nod
To get a Yes
From you
I try to impress
With my stupid mess
I did it back
I do it now
All for you

I try to give the signs
That I want
To make you mine
As I look at you
I try hard to define
I try hard to combine
All my feelings for you

I try to align
I try to confine

My gestures
My actions
My feelings that brew
I try to suffice
I try to concise
My emotions
My views
In front of you

I think of different ways
I plan as per the case
To dine with you
To get near you
In my stupid design
But then everyday
In the end
I try to convey
My feelings
With some trite
Romantic lines

Embracing the End

Not every time
The heart of mine
Calls out for you
But it does seek
Your love
Your care
Your affection
Your attention
For it requires
The support of this tryst
To climb up
The downhill
By holding your hand

And though my eyes waited
For an appraisal
From your side
To extinguish the pain inside
They never saw you
When I was in blue
And never did they find
A shoulder
On which they can rest
They can molder
And wipe these waters
Of emotions

And I understand
That it is better
To embrace the end
For my attempts
My efforts

To mend
Cannot fend
Cannot heal
The wounds inside me
But brings contempt
And I cannot pretend
To appear good
Appear fine
For somewhere
Down the line
I am hurt
I am burnt
Because of the expectations
I had for you
And the only thing
I remember now is
You were never there
When I needed you

The lost Dog

In a moribund ground of dirt
The gravel slowly quivered
And emerged from the slime
Two eyes covered in grime
Famished, withered
Two hungry eyes
Peered high
Into the endless skies
To find the rays
The bright rays
That can help him retrace
His missing friends
His loving family
His lost habitat
His own land

Rusted, Busted
The frail body lurked around
But his family, his land
Was nowhere to be found
The land, the faces
Which he once knew
Were all lost in the place
Which was certainly new

He tried hard to listen
But no sound did he hear
He tried hard to see
But nobody did he find near
Disillusioned with the loss
He still scans the places
He searches for the lost love

In the most callous faces
He tries to be presentable
He peers into the eyes
He waits shamelessly
For somebody to apprise
That he still can find the love
The love that is lost
He can still be accepted
With all his flaws

Thus
Despite being abused
He still waits
He still wags his tail
He still follows the trail

Shadows without light

In the dark room
I form the figures from shadows
The shadows of the dark
The shadows without a mark
I know they don't exist
But still I believe
And communicate
For they always make me think
That there lies inside them
A light where I can see
The silhouettes become figures
The contours become faces

But when I move closer
And try to touch them
They disappear
For they were never there
They were just a pretense
A false presence
I professed my eyes to believe
I bilked my senses to feel

But blame me not
for drawing these pictures in dark.
It's in this dark
This absence of light
The light appears more dominating
More enticing
More blinding
And being a blind
And somewhat adamant misfit

I keep on finding the hands
The hands that never existed

So I am delusional
For I see illusions
Without light
But then
Doesn't living in dark
Make a man delusional
A complete misfit

Think over it

The Pendulum

Like a pendulum
This life of mine
Swings
Between different phases
Different sections
Of this wordy world
A complexion
A collection
Of different colors
Different reflections
Which gifts
New connections
But brings
Dire dejections

Like a pendulum
This life of mine
Swings
Between cordial relations
And bitter wrangles
And I feel myself
Completely entangled
Between the euphoric highs
And the strained lows
Bringing hopes
Mixed with blows
Giving me a dose
Of no mediocrity
But extremity
As I fade
While I wade
Facing such intensity.

Strange is this life
Stranger is its motion
Which though is uniform
But is out of proportion
Sometimes
It showers upon you
Fountains of affections
And other times
It puts forward
A book of questions
And like a pendulum
This life of mine
Keeps swinging
And swinging
To and fro
And my mind
Keeps clinging
But doesn't rest
As it couldn't
Silently flow

Compassion

Often
In a rush
To reach my place
I gush
I chase the time
With a tremendous pace
Often paying no attention
No heed
To help the other
In need

But there are times
When I really want to halt
I really want to help
I really want to expand
My helping hand
I really want to nurse
Their wounds, their curse
I really want to reverse
Their phase of worse

I want to empathize
For my heart sympathize
With their suffering
Their miseries
But for reasons unknown
My well-built muscles
Cannot move
To improve
The conditions
The circumstances
The scenes

In front of me
And all I do
Is to show sympathy
To display a pity
On their hapless positions

It's not true
To term myself
Callous or brute
I am not completely
Impermeable
Inexorable
Or total astute
In fact
I see myself
As a good human
A good, noble, average person
But with this attitude
I do worsen
The respect
I've for myself

And thus
This inability
To substitute
My sympathy
With compassion
Makes me feel
A little inferior
In my own eyes
As in the end
It is always
The virtue of passion
The action of compassion
That makes one
Do something substantial

Twig of hope

Stuck in muck
I see my frail body travailing
Slowly yet boisterously
To reach out for a twig
A twig of hope that's weak
A twig holding scope yet bleak
Only to disappear and reappear
Countless times
In a continuous vicious circle
Each time toying with my feelings
Playing with my emotions

This twig
This optimistic stick
Shows some light
To my hopeless heart
That asks, calls and drives
My hapless body to follow
A shoal so hollow
In vain
Accruing the pain
For it fails
When this frail heart
With each futile attempt
Smolders to reduce
Into ashen ashes
And sitting at a corner
Immobile and still
I witness the horror
Of my demise
My end
With these two eyes

The Ship

I stand on the shore
Observing the chore
Of the captain
Of my ship
The ship of schemes
The ship of dreams
Whom I expect
Will take an audacious course
To simmer the waves coarse
Whom I presume
Will follow a definite path
A path following the heart
To mute the hoarse days
Whom I think
Will tackle the obstacles of sorrow
Will bring out a better tomorrow
That I can see every time
In these waves of hopes
When I come to the shore

But as I pack my luggage
And prepare to board
The miracle machine
Of dreams
I see a distant
Frail trail of the ship
Disappearing in the vastness
Of the ocean of my hope
Leaving me behind
Alone in the wilderness
Of my perennial agony

Maze

Polluted with confusion
Convoluted with delusion
The twisted lanes
In my twisted brain
Often twist and turn
Around no smooth curve
And all this dangling cart does
Is to tangle hard
And wrangle rough
To find a way out
From the hoarse gruff
But no paths become defined
No roads become aligned
No lane becomes a way
But everything ends up in affray

Heavy mist of ambivalence
Then settles down on the lanes
The roads become slippery
And all the directions wane
The dangling cart then entangles
In permutations of complex angles
And it is then gradually
But painfully realized
That the entire map
Once defined and clear
Is now covered and blurred
In a mist of heavy daze
And my innocuous and refined brain
Is now a complex and undefined maze

Dead Silence

There is a silence
A dead, awkward silence
Occupying every corner
Of my room
There is an aroma
A sad, gloomy aroma
Spreading everywhere
Of unusual gloom
And in this muteness
There is a strange blend
Of the frightful sounds
The tick tocks
Of the wall clock
And the beats
Of my heart
Clinking
Chinking
Exploding my ears
Bursting my head

But strangely enough
In this din
I am frightened
I am quiet in dread
For I feel dead
Daunted
Haunted
By this silent screeches
The agonizing
Horrifying shouts
Ripping off my heart

And all I do
Is to wait
For the light
To end the night

But when I know
I already know the right
It becomes onerous
To overcome the plight
In this tormenting
Dead silence

Breaking Dependency

Sometimes
All we need
Is a heart to believe
That it can achieve
The little joys
It always desires for
The little dreams
It always aspires for

Sometimes
All we need
Is a little courage
To embark
upon new ways
And obliterate
The dark days
By filling them
With illustrious rays

Sometimes
All we need
Is a single step
That eventually will make
Us live life
The way we want it to be

Sometimes
All we need
Is a little confidence
That eventually will break
All the shackles

And let us fly
Completely free

Sometimes
All we need
Is a little dose
That makes us tough
enough to cross the sea
And ultimately find
Happiness, the way we see

So I take this first step
And break all the chains
Of dependency
which holds back
My joys, my felicity
I unlock these fetters
To live life better
Which is graced with
the sense of simplicity
I work free
In the direction
To resolve my life
And remove the complexity
I love myself
And try to reconstruct
The genial ambience
Full with amity

And no longer
I am a bound man
For I will do
whatever my heart says
I will kill all the daze
And will fulfill my small desires
With these bright days

Now, in this moment
As I have killed
Dependency inside me
And I am relieved
To be free

The Lost epoch

Yes
I have lost the vigor
Yes
My limbs are now weak
Yes
My heart is palpable
Yes
Vestiges of hopes are bleak

Yes
The personality is dented
Yes
Energies are now faded
Yes
My psyche is demented
Yes
This soul is now jaded

Yes
Recuperation is now oblique
Yes
Bruised heart lacks the zest
Yes
The visions of love now leak
Yes
This heart can't give any test

Yes
The lost epoch
Brings the memories
Breaking
Shattering

My already battered
Grey soul
But No
I can't efface
The indelible
Signs of past
For they are still
As white as snow
Over the veil
Of memories
That remains
Like an ironical shadow
With me
During every new journey

Stranded

They make promises
To hold your hand
To walk alongside
Till the end
They make oaths
To be there
With you forever
Like a best friend

They make commitments
To be your vision
To be your light
To fend and transform
The dark sides bright
They assures their presence
Their support
To stand there with you
To be your hope
To love you
In the deplorable sights
With all the might

And then
When you start believing
Start falling
For the warm
Magical charm of theirs
You no longer
Remain a priority
But become a mere entity
And the treaty
To make us complete

Becomes obsolete
And you search
Here and there
For your individuality
Whose authority
Is no longer yours
But theirs

The hopes then
Strangle
The life
Entangles
In the webs of dejection
Depression
A callous ignorance
For you are left
Stranded
In the middle of a promise
That was never meant
To be fulfilled
But still your eyes
Wishes
That these promises come true
Like soprano dreams
Passing by

Fatal Ways

These ways
Say
Don't follow me
You'll shatter
You'll break
You'll die
But still
They charm me
They captivate me
To vehemently try
To willingly die
As
In these lanes
These perilous ways
There stays
A silver lining
A dole
For my soul
A way
To the ultimate goal
The goal
My soul is looking for
My heart is beating for

I, thus
Ignore the warnings
Of my inevitable predicament
And silently cement
A place
A space
For my grave
Where I'll rest

Every time I break
Every time I perish
In these
All important
All beautiful
But fatal ways

Mind and Heart

The clock shows 2
As I lie down on my bed
Conflicted, Dejected
My soul is all sad
Trapped between the notions
Of right and wrong
I feel churned
In this chaotic song

The stage is all set
The battle lines are drawn
The belligerents are present
To mercilessly maul

Introducing
The first belligerent
The ever working Mind
Practical, full of logic
Adamantly grinds me
Why can't you forget her?
And move on
Why do you still fear?
When she is not yours
Why don't you move ahead?
And live your life
Why do you fray yourself?
And slew with this knife

It explains
Life is big
There will be many roads
Why do you chain yourself?

Write yourself an ode
Why can't you divert yourself?
And keep yourself alive
Don't waste life in tears
Just leap and dive

But the other contender
The frail yet domineering Heart
Replies with a lament
In shrill cries
And announces that
It has tried
And even cried
But always has lied to me
That it can move on

Thus it stalks
The forlorn territories of hope
When my body is paralyzed
And it cannot even walk
While this heart has taken,
At most of the times
A sojourn of optimism

The heart declares
It might do anything
Good or bad
But without her
It's pale, it's dead
It may ride a tide
To cover its grief
But never can it be more
Than a dead leaf

And it may write an ode
But it can never bode

For life can never be same
When one is parted
From one's node

Thus
It tells the mind that
Even if you are rational
Even if you are practical
It cannot go your way
To make its day
For the life where
There is no her
Is nothing
More than hay

The battle intensifies
And I am torn
Assertions rise
And arguments fall
In this tirade
I being tired
Close my eyes and retreat
To meet my life
To meet her
To see a dream
To see a dream of her

And thus
I take a leap
And I sleep

Slaughter of 'Beef'

Waiting for her end
Her hapless
Helpless eyes
Are impassive
To shock of terror
The ultimate horror
That surrounds her
In a grisly macabre

She tries
But then succumbs
For she knows
There is no hope
There is no mercy
In the turpitude attitude
Determined to conclude
Her life in a plate

She might think
Why is she on the brink?
To meet her fate
When she didn't hate
The existence of others
She might contemplate
What did she do wrong?
Why didn't she belong?
To a community
That can live free

And when the blade
Does the carnage
She screams

Feeling the pain
Of the last stage
With her eyes
With the remaining life
Possibly thinking
That she might live
She might love
In her afterlife

An Unimportant Man

Having suffered many a blow
Even the stalwarts tend to feel low
Confidence shatters and dejections grow
When the charioteers fail
To put up a show

When the men of strength
Couldn't pull themselves up
Then how can I?
A simple, insignificant
An unimportant, non-existent man
Can show up
After being drubbed

I have failed and I am low
This is a fact I know
The lights I see are too dim
No rooms of life now aglow

My wounds are green
I am continuously being rubbed
In a world that doesn't empathise
I am kept being scrubbed
But who will notice
The throes that persist
For I don't exist
I hold no office

A single ray of light
A single feat of delight
Still I long for
Still I believe

Can set me alight
Can make me fight
All the odds
All the blots
For I know that I posses
The ingredients to progress
In a world
Occupied by the people
Important, significant people
I see akin to my skin

Heavy Heart

Sealed lips
Would not speak
The silent language
Of the heart
That connects us together
In a promise
To walk forever
Hand in hand
Till the end

But then
I realize
The journey
Was never too long
To make the moments chime
The bridges
Were never too strong
To seize the fleeting time

And eventually
I realize
It's the time now
For me
For thou
To empathize
The sand has slipped
Out of hand
The time has come
To embrace the end

And though there have been
Numerous mishaps

Multiple complains
But still they all look meager
When compared with this pain
This evil
Incomparable
Inevitable pain
To say goodbye
With the brimful eyes
With the heavy heart

Revenge

My blood boils
The sea of wrath roils
Whenever the sights
The memories
Hit me
Fiercely
With all the might
Returning the blight
The pains deep inside
Which reside
Which persist
All over me
Like a permanent stain

The blistering pain
Scalds me in this dormant
Fire of ire
And this hate
From the terrible burns
Creates
The hunger of revenge
The lust to avenge
For all the gloom
All the suffering
You brought to me

This hate
Brings more malice
More venom
In this callous body
Craving to be sadist
Bringing the diagnostic sign

Of caustic bitterness
This body is now
Brimmed with

But for whom is my revenge?
Who really suffers here?
I take this tough call
And then whip myself
With the same iron ball
The same scourge
I try to hit you with
And it retaliates and grips me
It's me who cries
Then in pain
For the soul dies
Every now and again

And the revenge
I sought for you
Ditches me
For it can never be true
For it always have risen
From the roots of sadness
That is somewhere adulterated
With the feeling of love
And affection
Still brewing
Inside my torn heart

Bags Packed

Relying on your gestures
Your words
Spoken or unspoken
Your promises
Made or unmade
Realized or proposed
I packed my bags
To elope the world
And walk with you
To the place
Where there is peace
There is love
Unbridled
Ungoverned by anyone

With a glimmer of hope
As I packed everything
To adorn our frame
Of beautiful dreams
I've lived in my eyes
Always with you
I waited for you
To walk those alien ways
Only to find
You to never come
Never arrive
Never comfort
In the desired drive

I see people
Rather passengers
Boarding

The cars, the wagons
Doing their thing
As I sit there
Waiting
Sometimes patiently
Sometimes impatiently
For you to come
With my bags packed

Voice

I am your anger
Your frustration
I am a dagger
Of your irritation
I am your dream
In apprehensions
I am a scream
In your dejections
I am your contempt
Your dissatisfaction
For the authorized
Established factions
But I am leashed
I am bound
I may shout
Without making any sound
For I am an entity
Obscured in your identity
Trying to surface
But unable to rebound

So you decide
Whether you want to implode
Everyday inside
Or explode once
To be free
To discover the hidden facets
The alien, brighter sides
And to give your voice
Finally some sound
That can be heard aloud

Enlightenment

Often in life
We circumvolve
Over the notion
Of rights and wrongs
And thus the thirst
For the nectar of peace
Always prolongs

And we experience
The roundabout turbulence
That eventually becomes
Our entire circumference
As we always look to
Escalate our conscious
Be righteous
And thus the soul searchers
Even didn't mind
To go completely abstentious

But in this devious approach
Soul searchers often neglect
The importance
Of knowing oneself
Of enlightenment
Of self-realization
About the things of enticement
That can make a person
Feel full
Feel high
Feel free
Like a bird in sky

For relishing is refining
For cherishing is defining
And no other thing is
More determining
In a person's success
In his ultimate shining
For it is imperative
To be fueled
With glee and felicity
To quench the thirst of soul
To attain a mortal's ultimate goal

The paths may be simple
Or they may be tough
But once the soul is fueled
With all its stuff
It will ascend
It will rise
It will ascend
To the ultimate prize

Even Buddha
The greatest
The holiest
Needed Paayasa
To attain boddhisatva
To reach enlightenment
So how can us, mere mortals
Can succeed on ruminating
Over stringent lines
Without excitement

I don't say
That being happy
Being satisfied
Will make everything possible

Will make transience permanent
But surely it will be plausible
To immune oneself from dent
For it will provide strength
The power
To cope from the loss
And rise to the vertex
The acme
As the fueled soul
When fired with ire
Of confidence
Of prudence
Can traverse any distance
Can subdue any resistance
And then it will be a stilt
To cover the wilt
To make life living worth
On this planet earth

Gaze

The lowered gaze
With a subtle smile
Comprise
Few vivid
Few wicked
Dreams
Protected
Fostered
In these
Somewhat timid
Deep eyes
Which tend to escape
To the cape
Of my own wishes
Where I am the queen
I am the duchess

And amid this atmosphere
I still adhere
To a hope
That someday
Somebody will come
That someday
Somebody will look
Into these eyes
And realize
The feelings
The meanings
Hidden in these
Lowered eyes

Quotes

Walking through the arcade
of this colorful life
I often look over
Beautiful messages
Appealing thoughts
adjuring us
exhorting us
To be strong
And believe in the character
The strength in character
That is enough to parry any scheme
Any plot
Plotted against us

I see quotes
I see notes
of notable men
Which brings to light
The insights
of these great souls
About truth, about life
About winning over the strife
In order to help us cove
And cover the flaws
The potholes
In the paths of our lives
Our characters

I find noble people
Charismatic abettors
Encouraging me
To believe in the visions of truth

The truth lying in ourselves
That will be the key to shackles
To withstand
the dejections
And to forget worries
Violent agonies
But enjoy thrills
the life has in store
and relax, chill.

But is it so easy
To kill the agony
That annealed our brittle hearts
Is it so simple
To extinguish
The burns we live with
which proliferates
On every wrong turn
Wrong turn to amend
To vanquish
Our fears
with supreme might
Of the preached character

No
It isn't a simple game
For our scars are permanent
They have seared long enough
To make the marks of crimson
On our psyche
And our psyche
Has something to blame
On our incompatibilities to cover
These scars of blades
Oh! What a shame

Thus
In a hope
To learn,
To develop
Some concerns
We walk the aisle
Where there are
Blind turns with
Sure death waiting for us

And we hope
That in this journey
On the unbridled path of experience
We'll find ourselves
And discover a true meaning
Of these quotes
In order
To get a better return
To flush our ashen
memories off urn
And truly exemplify
These quotes of courage
By living them with our own eyes

Delete your memories

Take away with you
Your memories
And set me free
From the ruins
Of your remembrance
For I cannot endure
The degree of misery
They bring
In the form of agony
Tormenting me
Every single day

Every single second
I am alone
I cannot hold on
Any more on the promises
To be strong
To be a stone
But I continue to moan
As I am now prone
To the attacks
Of those pinching
Flinching memories

I do try
To keep myself busy
Self-occupied with things
Stupid and inane
To be away from you
But what should I do
When my mind
Is already preoccupied

With the things
That bring back
The black
In my life

Though I am alive
But I couldn't survive
Fighting day and night
To revive
To Replenish
My dire, gloomy life
And the more I try
The more I fail
To obliterate these lines
To cover my cries

Thus please
Delete these memories
And leave my stubborn mind
Clinging to you, forever
For I want to recover
From the burns
Of your memories
Which have for now
Taken away
The peace from my heart
The soul from my soul
For you were my heart and soul

It's cold

In a din
I hear voices
Sounds, screeches
I hear noises
But unable to understand any
I hold a pretense
I camouflage myself
I present a pale countenance
For this world
Is a lot different
From the world of my dreams
Things here
Do not align
With the lines of my schemes
Is everything a riddle?
Presented in cipher?
Or is there a bug in my mind?
Opting to differ?

I ruminate often
And often I exhaust
I wander often
And often I get lost
But I find no door
To the questions in rife
I find no exit
From this indefinable strife
And the dregs of my life
Rustle anew
Always to end up
Getting mixed with blue
A blue mist

Devoid of any concrete gist
Any concrete answers
But questions manifold
A grim dorm
Where my smile is warm
But my heart is cold
An enigmatic cross-section
Where I follow the directions
But my way is lost

Damsel

In these flashy lights
Poignant sounds
I cease to elude
In an alien world
A world exclusive to me
Where I tend to ease
Where I sway in the breeze
In an aura of aroha
I find myself pampered
Fondled by a beautiful feel
A feel
I cannot describe
But sense
And fall in love with

And no matter
How many false gestures
I've to make
How many plastic smiles
I've to wear
I feel free
For I know
There is a realm
Into which I can slide
I can glide
And feel myself
Without the shams of snide
For I hold a key
To this glee
Where I can be me
Not the wretched mortal
But a beautiful damsel

Confession of a Failure

I came up short
I simply lost
I missed my bout
My chance
To get through
To reach to my goal
I feel withered and fray
I feel shattered and grey
I am perplexed
As I sought for a way
But with these rusty limbs
I am led astray

I feel annoyed
I feel miffed
When I hear your words
As I am riffed
I understand the points you make
I know there are decisions to take
But it's difficult to smile
When I am broke with a quake

I feel helpless
The quotes useless
My body hapless
My life hopeless
As I have lost
I have failed
I cannot see anything
But see myself derailed
And no quilt of care
Seems to work

As my eyes are stuck
Around the blue
That plucks
The flesh of my hopes

I appreciate your concern
I appreciate your will
But understand this
Your words make me ill
And though your intent
May be good
I don't doubt it
But I am in no mood
To relive my failure
And accrue my agony
My torment

Amid this storm
The downfall
I have to brawl
To stand tall
And I feel sorry
For myself
That I missed the cut
The chance to live
My story of glory
My script of desire
But I also understand
This very well
That I have to keep
This fire alive, in flames
To retry and reattempt
My journey
To ascent

But as of now
Please, I request
Don't ask me questions
And make me sad
For amid this dread
I feel half dead
Leave me alone
Give me my peace
For I need time
To purge myself out
From this grease

A morning scene

Scattered like foam
Flowing like gossamer
These clouds
Some grey
Some brown
Moving up and down
All around
The crown
Of nonchalant
Unperturbed hills
At the periphery
Of the town
Fill the morning
With a verve
That serves
My tired eyes
My fagged body
With a perk
While I travel
To go to my daily work

Hermit

Downcast under
The clouds of grey
I sought out
To pave a way
To a closeted place
Where I can have
A secluded space
A place for me
Where there is no hurry
No worry
No deadlines
No calls
But just frolic
Pure rollick
Free falls

I dream
To preen
My vista
With the scene
Of dreams
The meadows of greens
With no expectation
To rise
But fascination
To guise
The tensions
The mundane gloom
That my heart
Morosely loom

The thought
Of living such a life
A hermit's life
Away from the flashy lights
Gives my heart
A joy
A tremendous lilt
But the lure
The fear
The obligations
The trap
Of the real world
Jilts this fantasy world
I still long for

Lore

The lore of my pen
Thou might read with allure
Thou may love it
Or ask me questions galore
Thou might be content
With the content
Of the yore
Or
Thou might adjure
To seek the truth ashore
The truth
The clear truth
The apparent truth
I abjure
But supplant with a version
Of truths that lure
Truths of denial

Sitting in the bog
Shamelessly
I don't stop
Filling the logs
But secure
These inane
These absurd
Versions of truth
Or pseudo truths
In the lore
That some might accept
And others might reject
As a reflection of reality
In some distant future

Gift

Life
A box of chocolates
A package of surprises
Eventful, Dynamic
Wonderful things it comprises
And this life gave to me
The most expensive
The most precious
Gift in form of you
For things never were
And never can be as beautiful
As they are with you

You are the reason
Behind the grin
On my chin
You are the light
That illuminates every din
You are the spark
That fuels me with fire
You are a treasure
More precious than a sapphire

Happiness which comes to me
With you around
Is priceless
It's beyond any dime
And do you know
This treasure of happiness
Is contained
In this beautiful time
When we talked

For hours and hours
And made this bond
Tenacious and strong

Trust me
This bond
It's serene, it's pure
Completely, absolutely right
Trust me
Nothing will go wrong
Trust me
It's a gift
That life gives you
Very rarely
And expect us to take and oblige
By acknowledging this present
Of the present

If given the supplement
Of nourishment
This Gift
This Bond
Will overcome every odd
Every blot
And eventually will show
Us the true light
The path which glows
With absolute delight
And no plague, no blight
Will ever tarnish the shine
Of this beautiful thread
Between your heart and mine

Till then,
With a hope
That one day

One day
You will see
Things with my eyes
And understand this gift
That will make
Everything appears fine
I will wait

Lava

Listen to the clamor
The strident uproar
Roiling
Broiling
Inside
Like a lava
Ready to burst
Ready to erupt
To disrupt
Your dormancy
To wake you up
From your latency
And stir your mind
Flood your sense
To commence
To set yourself
In motion
With the notion
To make
To live
The presence
Of the top drawer
And not another brawler

You are not common
You are a dynasty
You are a reservoir
Of enormous capacity
And it is your potential
Your capability
That will never let you rest
Or embrace this false peace

Of complacent inactivity
But push you
Harder and harder
To the limits
Of your ability
For this lava
Will settle only
When you claim your position
When you make your hold
In the society
And make a name for yourself
In the pages of history
As someone worth
As someone known

Skies

The skies above my head
I am sure
They are the same above you
You would also see
The same stars
That here my little eyes do
The wind that touches me
I know it touches you too
For it tells me about you
The moon you see
I know he looks at you
For he can't hide his blushing hue

Peep out of your window
Out of those window bars
Look up at the sky
At those twinkling stars
Suspend once, for me those fears
Those old scars
The sky is not yours alone
But ours

In these twinkling lights
I try to frame your name
I do it here again and again
In these gloaming nights
I try to draw your face
Your smile takes away all the pain
Could you see those signs?
I draw in stars for you
Projecting your image in skies
Could you see those lines?

The words of love so true
The love that never dies

Peep out of your window
Out of those window bars
Look up at the sky
At those twinkling stars
Suspend once, for me those fears
Those old scars
The sky is not yours alone
But ours

You're in the other world, I know
But the skies above are same
The horizons have become too small
For I've written all over it, your name
Lift your head and smile just once
Give me a chance to see your face
Or just see the stars to the west
You'll find your picture
All over the skies
All over the place

The skies above my head
I am sure
They are the same above you
With the same pictures
I've made for you

Swag

Fettered mind
Unstable
Yet one of a kind
Draws the contour
Only to find
The silhouette of his self
Inked with an ink
Of excessive adulation
Of dangerous admiration
Which he foolishly thinks
As some transient salvation
In a transient world
Of swank and pride
Of shameless swag
Of pernicious avarice

Despite knowing
That his amble is a ramble
It's a trap, a gamble
A fallacy, a fake
A bog but no tranquil lake
A lake of peace
Tranquil and serene
He voluntarily swims
In the viscid waters
Only to sink
In a swamp of despair
Where his original
Genuine colors of self are all
But lost
And the shams of greed
A characteristic of this world

The world he abhors
The world he detests
Is now his flashy costume
In the flashy world

When You're Gone

Without any knock
Any footfall or voice
You stealthily
Quietly
Permeated this soul
And aromatized this body
With your lovely essence
That still lingers
Still holds and connects
My heart with yours
Even when you're gone

In these dark nights
When your dreams arrive
This soul is revived
I feel alive
But when the eyes open
You are lost
You retreat back to memories
But your lovely essence
Still lingers
Still holds and connects
My heart with yours
Even when you're gone

In these long passages
I find the echo
Of your lovely voice
Coming to me
Filling my heart to brim
And I automatically see you
For your image exists

Safely in my eyes
Even when it's lost
Somewhere in these vast skies
But your lovely essence
Still lingers
Still holds and connects
My heart with yours
Even when you're gone

Memories are revisited
Moments are pounded
My soul is kindled
My spirit is incited
The heart feels pain
When you leave me again
And disappear
In a place unknown to me
But it still feels like
You live inside me
As your lovely essence
Still lingers
Still holds and connects
My heart with yours
Even when you're gone

Shine of the Stars

Reclining in her chair,
She retired to a night oblique.
All black, the grim reflection
Contained no light, no streak

She impassively drew her to the outer window.
Resting her cold forehead against the cold glass.
She gazed at the waters flowing,
But saw no reflection in the dark.

The black envelope seized her with awe,
A melancholy of dire and sigh.
She looked cautiously through the glass,
But no cheerful image was in sight.

Her restive eyes followed the skies,
But found no shimmer in the calm.
Dangerously placid it occupied her quiet,
Creating thereby a disturbing bedlam.

The fright in her eyes,
Naturally caused her to shut the gateway.
The blocks were then blocked
And the new dark had no ray.

But a dusk emerged quietly,
Stealthily from the gallows of her heart.
Scruplously it lit the candle,
With the sparks of her guard.

The shimmers of her tender heart were seen,
As comets now in the envelope.

Mellifluous, her desires now flew,
Making a slow, gentle gallop.

The dreams bustled in the breeze,
Dreams which were arrested for long.
She quietly slipped into ease
From a taxing, oblique oblong.

The yearing eyes then opened her beautiful shutters,
And it gently gazed back to the night sky.
The shimmers now repalced the dark
For the stars were no longer shy.

She shouted out, aloud, her dreams,
All with her silent lips.
The skies of the dark, now arrested,
Fought hard to get her glimpse.

They twinkled and winked
At the beautiful her,
As she continued becoming aware.
They shone now more bright
With more might,
To catch the sight so rare.

And the medley of dreams,
Now was her smile,
Outshining the poor little stars,
That glowed all the while.

Finally the yearning eyes,
Looked again at the glass,
Now gently warm,
Looked at that figure of her,
And awestruck, they made her gasp.

How gorgeous she was,
And how brilliantly those eyes shone,
which she always knew, were a cozy, commodious home,
To the real beautiful self,
She saw now
In that beautiful reflection of glass,
Shining brightly
In the shine of the stars,
The stars of her eyes.

Foggy Night

Feeling groggy
In the foggy night
I crawl
In this dim light
I brawl
With the emotions
That take me high to the moon
As I stroll
In a hope
To get a text
Or a call
From you
Very soon

Slipping into the darkness
I continue walking aimless
Hearing the music
Of your voice
Muffling
All the city noise
I sing
The songs I never sang
I whistle
The tunes that never sprang
With the groggy feet
I walk
In a night
A lonely, dark
Foggy night
That appears so mine
So quiet
So blue

That it becomes imperative
It becomes causative
To expect
A sight
A sense
Or just a text
Or a call
From you

Room

My life story
My biography
I feel is confined
Within an enclosure
Of these few walls
People call Room
In which
These large images
The reflections of mine
Are loomed
In various shapes

In this giant room
All I see
Is an apparition
Of my spectral imagination
That keeps on changing
Wearing
The faces of illusion
I love to see
In an attempt
To bring a glee
To my gee looking face

In this huge room
In this colossal hall
I find the walls appalled
But decorated
With different textures
And shades
From the taints
And stains of blood
Out of my wounded

Quarantined, ruffled soul

It is in this room
I feel very alone
When this place
Grunts a solitary moan
Appears as a dead zone

It is in this room
I feel very alone
When the dead silence
Crawls and fills the air
And the only other sound
I can hear
Is the screeching squall
Is my shrill cry

It is in this vast room
I feel like my wings have curtailed
My aspirations chained
My advancements impeded
My freedom jailed

But still my eyes
Try to see
Beyond the wall
That stands tall
Still my heart
Tries to reach
To the voice of my call
And even being a captive
Of this imaginative
Lonely room
I try to be reactive
And dream
To evade
This hall of gloom

A mere dot

A single dot
What does it convey?
An ephemeral thought
Or a positive ray

I see it
As an initiation
As a source of light

I see it
As a salvation
From the despairing night

I see it
As an instrument
To make the mornings bright

I see it
As a start of line
To stop only at cloud nine
To rise and shine
To make everything fine

I see it
As the reason
To burgeon hope
To climb the rope

I see it
As a potent
Of endless scope

To break the barrier
To be a barrage
To be a harrier
To make the life large
I see it
Painting the azure sky
With the crayons
Of my imaginations
And making it possible
For a young dream
To break free and fly

As a brick is to a builder
A drop to an ocean
This dot could depict
Your life's way
Your script
For this mere dot
Engenders conducive thought
To stand, to resist
To fight any dreaded plot

It may be an end to some
To some a loss
But to me it's a vision
A vision if one follows
Makes him his own boss

Stones do melt

These eyes
With the passage of time
Had cried
On different lies
Had fallen
For promising disguise
Had comprised
Countless tears
Had experienced
Different fears
But I always knew
In order to rise
To improvise
I need to be wise
And thus made ties
With toughness
And made my heart
An impassive stone

But when the flashes
Of past
Of you
Of failures
Come to me
They haunt me
They daunt me
They thrust me
They push me back
In a track
Filled with aghast
Horror of terrors

Pains, scars, and infliction
I've risen from

And then
Even my so called tough skin
Becomes permeable
To these gushing emotions
And my heart of stone
Melts away
In this test
Of ultimate endurance
Making me thus a failure
I always was

Buddha

Buddha
The saint of saints
The center of centers
The tangent
To all the curvatures
He contains in him
Everything
The theories
The ambiguities
The congruencies
The true knowledge
Of this nature

Buddha
The Cognoscente
The Master
The ultimate sage
The ultimate pastor
He is the core
Of enticement
Of enlightenment
Of the real manifestation
Of truth, of life
For he sets out the lines
Which aren't stringent
Which aren't tough
But are practical
Are radical
Are marked
With mellowness
To cover our void
Our hollowness

Buddha
The Paragon
The complete soul
He sets an example
For generations
By being free
By being himself
By surrendering his desires
To the ultimate
And even in this generation
The virtue
Of knowing oneself truly
Helps one
To dodge the dogmas
To deceive the aversion
To be truly satisfied
By aborting contentions

And always
He stands there
Right above us
Calm and composed
Like a mellow orange sun
To guide us through
To pull us from
The paths full of burns
Into a world
Of purity
Of serenity
Where we can be ourselves
Where we can be true
Where we can feel
The eternity
We always wished to see

Peeping Eyes

Behind the bars
Inside some glass walls
Caged, jailed
Yearning eyes
Dream profoundly
To return back
To their original terrain
Their natural plane
Their natural lane
Away from any tether
Away from any chain

But the sane eyes
Refuses to look
Into their pain
As the intelligent
Homo sapiens
Choose to ignore
Their simple plea
Plea to live
Plea to live free
As captivity
Of ailed, inferior eyes
Seem normal
To our impassive
Superior eyes

Invisible Presence

Behind the curtains
Camouflaged
With a smile
Like an air
An invisible presence
I will be around you
I will see you
Not to ask anything
Not to want anything
But just to ensure
Whether you are
Safe and secured
Happy and zappy
And I promise
That I won't participate
But will volunteer
With an invisible hand
To protect you
To help you
To efface any of your fear
To wipe any of your tear
And to see you
Smile with glee
Till eternity

Glass or Steel

Glass or steel
What is my mold?
Frailty or anger
What do I hold?
Love or hate
What makes me strong?
Composure or Turbulence
Where do I belong?

Smile or frown
What keeps me down?
Red or white
What's the color of the crown?
Acceptance or Rebellion
What is my trait?
Success or dejection
What's written in my fate?

Answers lie deep within
But answers are all hidden
Are my actions right?
Are they justified?
Or are they wrong?
Completely falsified?
I cannot decode
For I cannot decide
What's the right road?
The right horse
On which I have to ride
To reach the dawn
What should be donned?
How should I correspond?

What should I shred?
What should I hold on?

And as I go on
Forward
The questions grow
So do the dilemmas
For I still cannot declare
If it is
Glass or Steel
The constituent of the mold
I have cast myself in.

Clown

Wearing a makeup
A pseudo smile
Covering myself in colors
I have made this a style

I apply red
I apply green
But you see me
Descent and clean

I am a gentleman
Outside
Emulating decency
Making a legacy
But I am a madman
Inside
Master of disguise
I raise your discrepancy

No one can understand me
No one can identify me
Because your eyes can't see
True colors of me

They see
Only what they think
What they predict
Making me a hero sometimes
And sometimes a convict

But they can never be true
They can never be just

For they are the slaves
Of their inner lust

I don't want your mercy
Nor your clemency
For an identification of me
In this world of exigency

You can't hold me
Indicate me
Designate me
Discriminate me
On the basis of my color
My race
My caste
My face

For I am now defaced
Camouflaged
And no matter
How hard you try
You cannot surface
The true self
Which I hide from you
Behind this face

You may look up
The entire town
And you can never know
Whether I am red
Or brown
You may try
You may frown
But you will always
Be let down

Because I am faceless
I am a clown
And you can never identify
The true me
Whenever I am around

Flower of Gloom

Screeches
Screams
Shrill Cries
Broken Dreams
Are not something new
They are something
That have already made
My life blue
For they always have
Been a part
An integral part of myself
And never in future
Will be apart
From the conscious self
But this excruciating pain
Which I endure
Again and again
Has nourished continuously
A flower of gloom
That was born
On the very first day
Of my then approaching doom

And since then
I have been tattered
I have been rattled
I have been worn out
As day and night I battled
To remove the seed
Of weed of throes
But this flower
Continued to grow

Continued to rise
As it got the nourishment
The supplement
Of somber demise

And today
Albeit
I sustain my fight
Against the hardships
Against the plights
It really doesn't matter
For this wanton weed
This flower with blood petals
Has accede to the throne
As now it has acquired
All it's might
All the nutrition
From my own crimson
Which it leeched
From this body of blight

And I know now
It is a part of me
An inevitable evil
An indispensible mate
So it bothers me less
As my life is a mess
For I know
My efforts to prune out
This small seedling is futile
For it will always bloom
For it is now
A Flower of Gloom

Drafts

Wrapped in the scraps
I stumbled upon the drafts
Intuitive collection
Of some undelivered crafts
Containing in them
A projection of insanity
A tirade of profanity
Desperation for vanity
Reflection of personality

I saw in them
A wrecking mayhem
Of gushing wrath
And sometimes
An attempt to recover
From the aftermath
A tiring attempt
To convince my heart
Or an emotional passage
To win your heart
I saw in them
A call to start
To create my own art
A gamble to cheat
The games of darts
With you as the ultimate prize

I saw the various emotions
With varying intensity
Of maturity
Of elasticity
Of pain

Of desperation
To mend and append
The broken porcelain
Of my fragile
But agile heart

I revisited the history
Written by my own hands
Which I buried in past
Under the beds of sands
And I saw in these pages
Different images
Of the most secured
Most obscured
Sometimes authentic
Sometimes crazy
Pictures of my
Sane and Insane
Personality

Black or White

Thousand theories
One solution
Either Black or White
Will give me a respite
From the million thoughts
Running day and night
In my tumultuous head
Gradually eating me up
Like a plague
Like a blight
Abducting my will
Making me dead

I am tired of believing
The glare of neon lights
I am tired of assuming
The colors of sights
I am sick of suspecting
The conspiracies that hold
I am sick of expecting
I just want to be bold.

Perspicuity is all
I look for
I long for
And it doesn't matter now
If I were a bait
But sure I cannot wait
To look over the hints
Work over the clues
To solve a jigsaw
From the answer I choose

I look for clear answers
A defined, specific path
For it's the clarity
That shall clear the mist
That shall assuage my wrath

I don't wish to dodge
These dogmas any more
I don't wish to toss
These hoaxes any more
As I want to see this
Either in Black or in White
I am tired of sustaining
My everlasting fight

I have realized
The roads, the ways
The answers, the greys
Black or White
They have to be

And I don't care
If these answers bring me
Some sort of gloom or doom
All I care now about
Is leaving no room
For these caustic uncertainties
These manipulating greys
To manipulate me further
But about restoring faith
In the vista of truth
That will empower me
To find the definition
That lies in me
In either black or in white

Train from your town

The hoots of the train
Coming from your town
Inform me
About your whereabouts
About your wellbeing
About your current life
About you, my love
And I snatch from them
The air you breathe
The dreams you see
The aroma you wear
Which I preserve
In the reserved section
Of my heart
Exclusive to you

As a token of respect
And a greeting of love
I wrap
My inclusive feelings
My reflexive blessings
In an air of love
That you have gifted me
And I parcel it
Back in the train
Going back to your town

Resolutions

Hundreds of promises
Millions of resolutions
I make to myself
Every day

Every day
I ask myself
To find a meaningful
Reason in life

Every day
I show myself
Wonderful quotes
To fight off the strife

Every day
I treat myself
With tempting delicacies
To add flavor in life

Every day
I try to play
My wildest fantasies
To add a little spice

With every morning ray
Every dawn of the day
I move out of hurdles
To make my way

I commence strongly
I advance confidently

Only to end up sinking more
In this chasm of romance

And when I hear the tocsin
I sense the asphyxiating toxin
I wake up in the bog
To find myself stuck

And the more I duck
The more I am pulled
Into the webs of my thoughts
Which once I mulled

I find absolutely no chance
To enhance my life
In this moor of pragmatism
But still remembering the notes
I fight to burgeon
Vulnerable buds of optimism

And in the end
When I am tired fighting off
The sinister inevitable
I end up enervated
Tired and hapless
More than ever

But my adamant self
Still refuses to say never
And it keeps on fighting
The odds forever

Being torn in this fray
I then forsake
The oath to be gay
Making all these promises

Commitments, resolutions
To be strong
To be brawn
Abortive

The Seat beside me

Racing trees
Browns and greens
Majestic, serene
These beautiful scenes
My eyes hold
In a dream
In which they see
They feel
They share
This feel
This beautiful feeling of love
Of life
With you
Only you

I feel the warmth
Tender warmth of your palm
Stroking my forehand
I hear things
Lovely things you said
Without even a word said
I feel the rush
The thrill from your hand
When you squeeze my hand
I feel your aroma
The ensnaring fragrance
In all the times I spend
With you
Only you

I sense your touch
Gentle touch of your fingers

When they play with my fingers
I experience that softness
The softness of your skin
When you rest it on my shin
I know your ruses
Your cute little pranks
When you blow that puff in my ears
I do feel your kiss
Sublime, surreal kiss
When you make me yours
And banish all your fears
I feel the moments
The beautiful memories
The times of mirth
The times of glee
I saw and still see
With you
Only you

When these rational brains
Living in a cerebral world
Wake me up
Call my name
To join them
In all their futile conversations
In their otiose discussions
And ask me to recite
Their handwritten script
That they have named as delight
I refuse to comply
I refuse to leave
My majestic show
For an unoccupied seat beside me
Adorned with delicate dreams
Still ensnares my mind
And I continue to relish my trek

My adventure
That I have lived
And I still live
With you
Only you

And these people
After writing a dissertation
Avow their declaration
That I am sad
I am depressed
But I chuckle for I know
The life I live in my eyes
In this trance
Is what I truly love
Without you physically present
But still
With you
Only you

No worries

Why strive
When you can thrive
Why duck
When you can strike
Why frown
When you can appreciate
Why wait
When you can initiate
Why hold
When you can release
Why scold
When you can please
Why impersonate
When you can be you
Why deviate
When you can pull yourself through
Why hate
When you can love with glee
Why sit back
When you can fly free
Why fight
When you can win with a smile
Why drag
When you can walk a mile
Why worry
About the dud and dunce
Why waste
The life that comes
Only once

Clueless

With a heavy heart
And a straight face
He stands there clueless
With an empty gaze
He watched the spring
Entering through gates
Only to escape
In a dreary daze
He stands there clueless
All alone
He's brutally shattered
He's all torn
He stands there clueless
On the thorns
He watches her smiles
Turn into scorn
Frantic at heart
Stoic at face
His heart beats out
With an incredible pace
Yet he stands clueless
Yet he waits
To witness his mark
Completely efface
Puzzled, Riddled
He stands there perplexed
When he should weep
His face seems relaxed
Amused, Confused
His heart is vexed
He stands there clueless
To watch himself axed

He hopes when there's no hope
He thinks when there's no scope
He wishes for a miracle
When there is no miracle to cope
Yet he stands clueless
To watch his dear lope
He watches her go
And disappear
He knows she's gone
She won't reappear
Yet he stands clueless
Clueless he waits
For a perennial stormy night
To finally abate

Tell me

Do tell me
If I can hold your hand
And make you cross
The seas of gloom

Do tell me
If I can be a friend
And listen to you
All night, all noon

Do tell me
If I can shut your eyes
And prevent you from
The thorns of lies

Do tell me
If I can show you dreams
And make you see
The beauty in life

Do tell me
If I can carry your weight
And hold you upright
In any storm in life

Do tell me
If I can be a latch
And hold you tight
In any dreary strife

Do tell me
If I can be a plane

And take you up
To the heights of moon

Do tell me
If I can be all sane
And describe you
The fables of bloom

Do tell me
If I can improve myself
And be a man
You always liked

Do tell me
If I can correct my wrongs
And be perfect
To fall in your line

Do tell me
If I can wear the smile
And don the costume
Of your choice

Do tell me
If I can be guiled
And speak your magic
In my voice

Do tell me
Do tell me once
If you ever need me
And I promise
Dear! I promise
I'll be there
I promise
For I always think of you

In every night of blue
For I always live with you
In every night of blue

You don't need to shout
A whimper will tell me
That you need me
And I promise
I'll pack the bags
And come to you
For I always think of you
In every night of blue

Do tell me
Do call me once
I plead
For my eyes bleed
To get a call
To hear a word
A single word
From you
My estranged love
For I wait for you
For I think of you
In every day of dark
In every night of blue

Disguise

Driven by a lure
Of a cure
In a form of hope
I dope
My senses with a belief
Of optimism
To get a quick relief
A lasting settlement
For my own betterment

Though I despise
The game of disguise
I keep rolling my eyes
I do surmise on the lines
On the clues
Of these tempting lies
In a hope
To apprise myself
Surprise myself
With a truth
I try to find
Beneath the cover of lies

I know
That this unsatisfied
Love seeking heart
Will throw tantrums
Will throw complains
Because it contains
A rage of tumult
Inside a slump
But still

It is ready to take a bump
For it still grows
Cherishes
And lives
On the crutches of hope
He cannot recognize
As genuine or disguise

And thus I keep fooling it
And in turn
I keep fooling myself

My Final Goodbye

I never thought
Saying goodbye
Will be that hard
For I believed
I have buried all the glum
All the faces of blue
I had in mind
Related to you
Somewhere
Deep
Inside the layers
Of my complex mind
But then
I find
It extremely difficult
To say a farewell
And pack the bags
To lead a new way
A new life
For somewhere
The present antipathy
You have for me
And I have for you
Chokes me
Croaks my movement
For there is no settlement
Of the rising tides
Which still do sweep me
My senses
And renders me immobile
Absolutely numb

And still somewhere
Inside the purlieus of my soul
There is this small desire
To speak out
All the love
I have for you
And make you mine
Or atleast
Restore the feelings
And make things work fine
The way it was
Between you and me
So that the cold looks
Are replaced by smiles
Whenever we look
Or even think
Of each other

And thus
It makes my throat dry
My limbs weak
My face pallid
My eyes wet
To move out
Of the vista
Without making the edges even
Without healing the wounds
And say to you
With the frazzled heart
My final Goodbye

Image

My history is not simple
It's written with twisted words
For twisted words
Can only describe
The amazing, baffling animal
Inside me
And turning back the pages
I too am perplexed
To see the complex gamut
Of roles and emotions
I've been tangled in
Always

I haven't been correct always
For I did many a mistake
When I failed to take and make
Apt decisions in different situations
And conclusions, thus
Have been also different
Sometimes making me win
And sometimes hurting me bad
Making my image tortuous
Just like my life is

Albeit I've been mad
And listened to inaudible sounds
And walked in invisible lights
I've made sure to weave
The allure of the sights
The magic, the charms
That this first
Surreal connection brought

And though I habitually
And hopelessly
See with my eyes closed
And weave with my hands bound
I am still aware of
The gravity of the real sound
That connection I try to make
Might break the barrage
Of dreams
These eyes preserve

I nevertheless
Ask for her hand
For I am too blinded
By the bright light
Of the hope in this connection
That I feel strongly
Is made for me
But I am also aware
That this probably will end up
Hurting me
Breaking me
And making my image
My life
More tortuous
More complex

A *funny man*

A funny man
He is so foolish
He makes mistakes
Receives aches
Learns lessons
But repeats them all again

A funny man
He is so foolish
He analyzes problems
He discovers solutions
He identifies answers
But doesn't write any of them

A funny man
He is so foolish
He scans empty pages
He inspects forlorn places
He realizes the void
But keeps searching same traces

A funny man
He is so foolish
He plans his days
He contrives his ways
He designs to get himself started
Before getting totally thwarted

A man of folly
A maverick buffoon
An eccentric loon
I see in my skin

Wearing my face and my colors
Residing in filthy gutters
Where I too live

But he doesn't die
Nor do I
He is a daydreamer
He is a procrastinator
He is an idealizer
He is a fantasizer
Just like me

Finding fun in the grit
Pleasure in the filth
Oh sure! He is a funny man
For he's too foolish
Too vapid
Just like me

Destitute

The dreamy yet dreary eyes
Of a hungry destitute
Often constitute
A morbid fear
When these pauper eyes
Aloof from the swank of the city
Are stuck on the drops dripping
From the roof of pity
And often these famished eyes
Contemplate on logic to apprise
The conscientious yet conscious self
About the luxuries of life

A cozy bed, and a balanced meal
His vivid imagery did steal
From the vistas of paradise
That are preserved in his eyes
But his wine is water
And his dinner is dust
As the dreamer continuously
Struggles to adjust
In a testing, acting life

Despite being tossed
In the hardships of life
He still is lost
To find the meaning in strife
For he believes
That life is a book
A book that teaches
A book that preaches
A man to survive

A man to thrive
And his condition is just a test
To prepare him for the fest
That is far above any material
But the vanities of surreal

He firmly believes
That this regress to distress
Is in fact
A catalyst to progress
To a world
Where he drops the screenings
But adopt the meanings
The multiple meanings of life

With a restored faith
He is then awake
From his open eyed slumber
By the trickling tumbler
But he is more resolute
Completely absolute
To lean and learn
To earn and yearn
In this life of a destitute
Enabling him to fully appreciate
The colors of life

Faithful Pain

That's the way
I have lived
That's the way
I possibly will
It has been my peer
It has been my pill
It has been loyal
It has been inseparable
It has been unavoidable
It is now forever

It stings me
It bites me
It kills me
But excites me
For it is the drug
That infuses the life in me
Paradoxically something
That no longer lies in me

Call me a freak
Call me plain weak
But my soul reeks
In the pleasure I seek
In the form of pain
That runs down my veins
As I know
It will never go
But will accompany me
Like a faithful bride
Till the last spot
To my last stop
My end

Bird of Death

Sitting in the bleak night
She sharpens her beak
Keeping her hold tight
She cackles a shriek

Her sinister cacophony
The characteristic of lore
Daunts the dreary night
Like never before

Her spooky mannerisms
The omen of plight
Forebode an inevitable tragedy
Disperses an eerie fright

Her smoldering eyes
The paraphernalia of blight
Glares at me continuously
Her prosaic face
The intimidating sight
Screams at me hysterically

But despite hiding myself
I unabashedly stare back
To me, she's a metaphor
Of a life that's already black

I breathe the omen
The signs of the plague
I am a prey to be hunted
I am a living dead

So tweak me with your beak
Kill me with your strike
I am just a shrimp
A delicacy for you, shrike
Give your best shot
Don't let me be alive
I am willing to surrender
To cease my life's strife

Traverse

Different distances I traverse
Different challenges I face
With new people
New companions
New phases I surface
New chapters turn up
New energies come up
New lives ask
To stand up
And fight against
That latent dormancy
And embrace
The different colors
The different shades
The multifaceted life
Contained in regency

But then in the plethora
Of different merry faces
The vista of mine reflection
Somewhat effaces
The hope I carry
Slowly undermines
And the old dents
Then determines
The character
The dented character
Which I paint
To appear better

And I return back
To the old

Dented and Demented self
Burning slowly
In the shallow fire
Set ablaze
Back in the black

Enchantress

I've always been bewitched
Captivated first and then ditched
By a tempting seductress
A dangerous enchantress
Who offers me often
Various aids to soften
The life that has become too marred
The strife that has become too hard
And enticed to see light
I too readily become beguiled

I foolishly think to follow
When my bosom is nearly hollow
And when I try to take a step
I am often taken aback
For my limbs are all weak
My strength is too bleak
But my mind still restless
Keeps thinking of the temptress

Blinded and paralyzed
I still keep waving my hands
But too numb I've become
I just cannot leave this land

And then when I sit down
Withered and dilapidated
This seductive temptress returns
This time more animated
And again she offers me her aid
Again she asks me to evade
And despite being withered

I believe her
I crusade
In this cycle of nothingness
I inadvertently fade

Flight

Oh young bird
Just for once
Close your eyes
Shut your senses
From wrongs and rights
Listen to the sounds
The sounds of the breeze
Feel yourself flowing
In the limitless with ease
Close your eyes
And see that sky once
Let the tears trickle
And kill the fear at once
Oh young bird
Sign of juvenile
Realize your dream
To freely run a mile

Oh young bird
Just for once
Listen to your heart
Don't judge
Don't predict
But indulge
In the pleasure of art
Feel yourself as the one
The one in your dreams
Cleanse yourself, just for once
In the gleam of their sheens
Oh young bird
Symbol of innocence

Fly high
Register your presence

Oh young bird
Just for once
Keep your palm on the chest
And experience the building thumps
Feel the beats of the heart
And let the muscles jovially pump
Groove with the rhythm of dreams
And let the music grow
Feel the rise in your energies
The energies that make you glow
Listen to the thumping heart
The thumping heart that calls
That shouts
To erase all the fears
And clear your doubts
Close your eyes
Oh young bird
Just for once
And let the real self
The real you
Come out

Oh young bird
Just for once
Believe
That no bond
No shackle
Can deceive
You from the course
Of that delight
I know
You know

You see in the light
The light visible
Only when
You close your eyes
The light visible
Only when
You traverse away from lies
To see that a bird
A young, innocent bird
Waits for the call
The call of the flight
To fly and realize
That the sky in front of him
His life, his dream
Can truly become his own
For it belongs to him

Your Eyes

These eyes of yours
Behind all this makeup
In an attempt to even up
In an attempt to hide
Those emotions
Still appear
A little familiar
A little eager
To speak out
Things inside you
In some obscured hope
That someone sneaks through
The barrier you had put
And understand this language
The dreams
That you still confide
That you still bide
In those wide
Deep but troubled eyes

And no matter
How much you avoid
How much you try
To dress them sangfroid
I see some turbulence
Some dejection
That was always present
That I always saw
In those eyes

But even as I understand
And try to offer my hand

I know
You have decided to go
Some alien land
In a hope
That this language
Will be comprehended
And appreciated
By someone else
But not me

A Dreamy traveller

A dreamy traveler in a logical world
He wanders the streets of love
He picks up the pebbles
He fills in his pockets
With these sweet testimonials of bluff

A dreamy traveler in a logical world
He prefers to walk in dark
He walks on these paths
He strolls in these lights
With the memories of her spark

A dreamy traveler in a logical world
He weaves this fabric of scheme
He embellishes this silk
He adorns this cloth
With the pearls of his dream

A dreamy traveler in a logical world
He preserves these wonderful sights
He revises the segments
He relives the figments
He saw once in an ethereal light

A dreamy traveler in a logical world
He listens to the words of joy
He recalls the phases
He reiterates the phrases
As a part of some clever ploy

A dreamy traveler in a logical world
He invades the black night

He watches the stars enact
He sees the sky project
The movie of his delight

A dreamy traveler in a logical world
He wakes up to the sirens of fact
Pragmatic calls, realistic truths
They disrupt his pleasure act

But without making much sense
The dreamy traveler crosses the fence
Of bitter realities
Thence return to the shore
The dreamy roads
Where he closes his eyes
And smiles on his wounds
The conformity of his pretense
Which now are his grounds
Where he strolls and hounds
The imagery of imaginations
The dreamy manifestations
All in her presence
Away
Far away
From the logical world
In which he has to inevitably return

Printed in the United States
By Bookmasters